MW01517161

books by
BOXER

www.booksbyboxer.com

Published by
Books By Boxer, Leeds, LS13 4BS UK
Books by Boxer (EU), Dublin D02 P593 IRELAND
© Books By Boxer 2022
All Rights Reserved
MADE IN CHINA
ISBN: 9781909732919

WILD GARDEN

A GUIDE TO A ~~GROWING~~ Neglected OASIS

WET ~~WILLIES~~ WELLIES

Been too lazy to bring your muddy wellies inside, and now your garden looks like a mouldy ShoeZone discount rack?

Not only do these boots really help to bring feng shui back to your garden, but they can also serve as great homes for frogs.

Like something from an episode of Benefits Britain, you too can have many (frog) families living rent-free in your garden! Call the bailiffs if you dare...

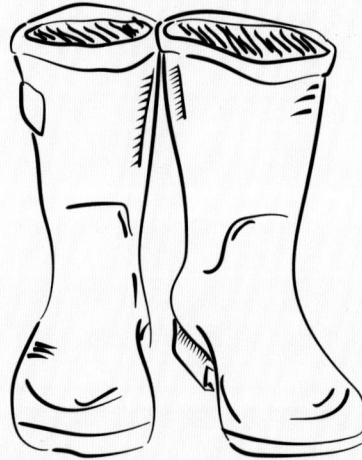

SKIP THE TRIM!

Body shaming is so 2021...so why trim your backyard bush?

Letting your bush grow can make a home for wildlife, such as spiders and worms, and makes a great sheltered nesting spot for birds and hedgehogs!

Remember, if your garden resembles a 70's porn flick, then your bush could be home to some cheeky critters and tits!

LEAVE YOUR HOLE OPEN

Has stormy weather left your garden fence looking like the Berlin Wall, post 1989?

If your fence is missing a few panels, not only does this open your garden up to your neighbours, doubling your outside space, a few gaps in your fence can also allow for a new high-speed hedgehog highway, planning permission not required!

BOUNCY SURPRISE

Ever looked outside your window after a storm and thought... when the f**k did I buy a trampoline?

If the wind blows one into your garden, don't call the council. Think of all the fun foxes could have spending their nights perfecting their trampolining routines.

If you keep this bouncy bit of equipment, soon local wildlife will be able to give the Chinese gymnastics team a run for their money!

RUG MUNCHER

You know what most gardens are missing these days? Carpet.

Old carpet scraps can really help to bring the inside-out, and make great insulated linings for ponds and flower beds.

Don't be too disheartened if your rug ends up covered in bird poo - your interior design choices aren't to everyone's taste.

BIN THERE DONE THAT!

Is your wheelie bin overflowing with pizza boxes and wine bottles?

Bin men not due for another week? Your outdoor haven is already looking like a pigsty, so drop the tidy neighbour act and use your garden as your own personal tip!

Last night's kebab in naan bread will make a tasty meal for crows today, dog food will feed hedgehogs, potato peels can help your soil, and you can piss off your neighbours all while looking after nature!

PUSHING UP DAISIES!

Pissed off with cold-callers knocking at your door, killing your vibe with their hopes of making you join their church or sign up for their crappy broadband?

Why not make your garden look like a serial-killers private cemetery! All you need to do is sit back and relax, G&T in hand, until your lawn (and buried bodies) start pushing up daisies.

No more pesky salesmen, and you'll be helping tired bees and ground-borne insects rest and take shelter too!

MOIST MOSS

Is your garden looking as dry as a nun's gusset? There's no need to be ashamed of your dusty lawn and droopy bushes... it happens to the best of us.

What you need is a low-maintenance option like moss! Basically a merkin for your garden, moss will help vajazzle up your bald patches, making your garden a vibrant wonderland that'll attract lots of attention from damp loving wildlife due to its moist nature.

Bonus: It'll never need mowing, and it might even bring all the boys to the yard!

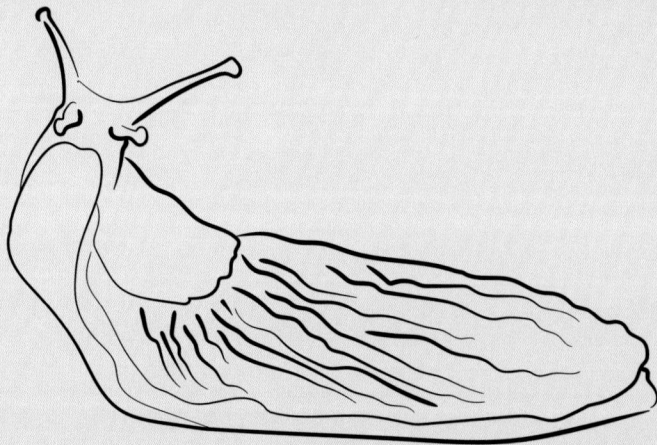

HEDGE-PIONAGE

Is Jeoff at number 17 having a fling with Irene down the road? Maybe you want to see how many Uber Eats Dave has a day? Stop being a curtain twitcher and grow yourself a bush!

Definitely not an obvious hiding place, you can roll around your garden like a budget James Bond, peeking through your bushes at your convenience in your devious act of espionage!

You'll be the gloater for gossip at your corner shop, and you'll help save some little tits and prickly friends along the way!

(You can call me Agent Bush)

WINO-GARDEN!

Doorstep looking like a wino's haven? Janet from number 47 giving you a dirty look and tutting as she passes your home? You're not an alchy, you're an advocate for nature!

Down those bottles of rosé and fill your garden with drink-inspired decorations.

Turn your booze into bricks to line your paths, or just leave them scattered around to fill with mucky rainwater... whatever tipples your fancy!

TYRED OF THE SAME OLD DÉCOR?

Got a few tired tyres laying around in your garden? Good job! Not only do these add a contemporary twist on garden décor, they look gorgeous all year round!

Perfectly paired with cigarette ends and crumpled bottles of Frosty Jacks, tyres are great for adding a contemporary feminine touch to your garden!

Whether you use them as a makeshift flowerbed, comfortable chair, or even leave them as a sculptural installation, old tyres are perfect for taking the yawn out of your lawn!

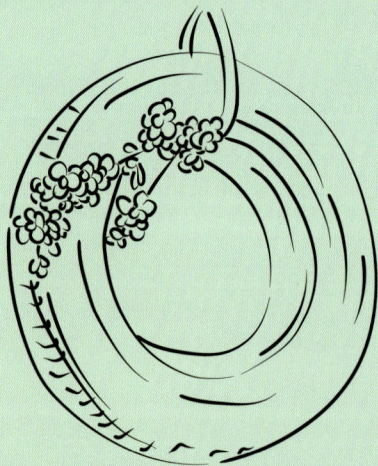

EGGCELLENT

Neighbour's kids been egging your house... yet again?! Follow this tip to get all the local ladies jealous at how quickly you can get your eggs fertilised!

Egg shells can be crushed and sprinkled onto soil to help act as a fertiliser for other plants - simply lob them out of your window and watch your garden transform from the garden of weed-en to the Garden of Eden!

HAVE A FRIDGE-D GARDEN!

Dragged your fridge outside one time for a BBQ in summer, and decided it looked better in your garden?
Well, you're not wrong!

A rusty fridge not only looks great as a modern garden feature, it also has many uses! Stand it upright for a makeshift shed, lay it on its back for a makeshift flower bed, or fill it with water to get a luxurious swimming pool!

It even comes with a jacuzzi-style lid to keep the water free from insects! All your neighbours will be jealous of your shiny new pool, but remember... no diving allowed!

HOLLY-WOOD

Treat yourself to a new wardrobe from Ikea? Is your old one now rotting away in your backyard?

You might have realised by now that only bikes and flower pots get nicked... don't worry though! The local scrap man might not want your soggy seconds, but creepy crawlies will!

Your favourite pile of wood will be the Hilton Hotel of your estate. VIP beetles, insects and grubs will take residency, and you might even bump into Kate Moth, Maggot Robbie or Snailer Swift!!

BIG STONER

Remember in the 80's when everyone had a pet rock? Lucky you, you have a garden full. So why not display your collection like Makka Pakka from In the Night Garden?

Not only will it make your garden look like the Stonehenge, it'll bring your neighbours, newts, and frogs joy too!

Bonus tip: Draw faces onto your stones and rocks to make it look like you have friends!

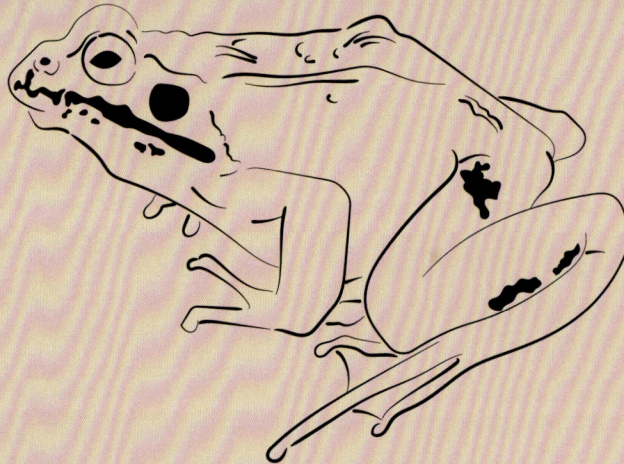

BASKET CASE

Banned from flying after an airport incident on your way to Shagaluf, and now have loads of empty suitcases lying around the gaff that you no longer need?

Worry not! Your dodgy airport antics may have left you with some unique flowerpots! Lined with fabric, suitcases can stay moist and warm, making them the ideal home for small flowers.

Drill holes in the bottom and use them as beds for small flowers, just remember to empty out your tanning oil and crusty thongs first!

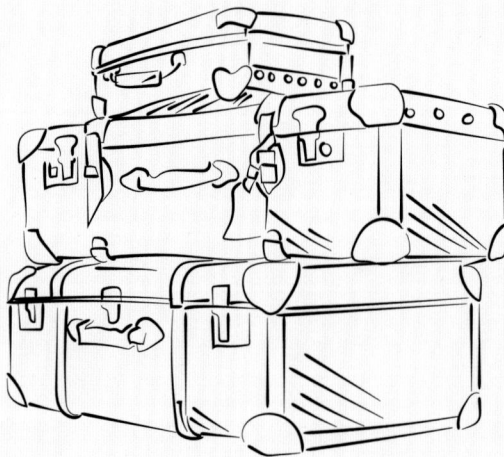

A BIT OF THE BUBBLY

Been wasting your paycheck on useless tack, and now find yourself drowning in bubble wrap?

Rather than shoving it in a neighbour's wheelie bin, this seemingly pointless bit of plastic can actually be good in your garden!

Wrapping it around your pots can keep your plants warm in the winter months!

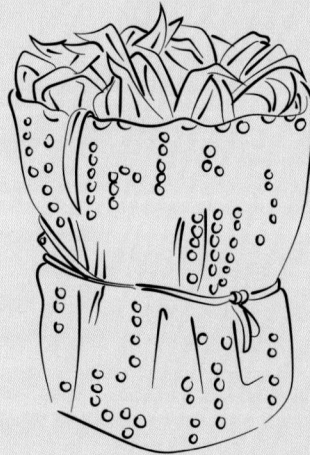

TURN YOUR GARDEN INTO A HAIRY TALE

Did you know that human hair is an effective natural fertiliser? Containing magnesium, hair can be shoved into soil or compost to help add support and nutrients.

So, next time you give yourself a cheeky Brazilian or back, sack and crack before a trip down to your local, remember to sprinkle your short and curlies onto your lawn!

WARNING: Don't let the neighbours see, you may get sectioned.

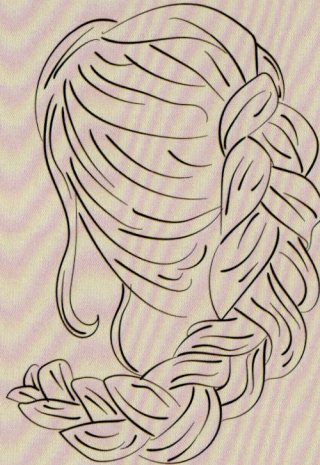

SHARING IS CARING

Has your back yard been magically growing rubbish, and you need a way to get rid of it? Perhaps you've been expanding your landscaping skills with empty tinnies and condom wrappers.

Fear not! Did you know that most houses come with at least one, if not more, large and accessible bins? Called 'The Neighbour's Garden', this mysterious bin can be used all throughout the year, and is a super effective way to clear your garden of trash!

FAKE IT TILL YOU MAKE IT!

Can't be arsed to look after real life flowers? Honestly - sometimes it's hard enough to look after yourself! Fear not, it's what plastic flowers were made for.

Shove them in the ground to add a pop of colour to your lawn. If they fade, who cares?! It's not like real flowers last forever either... dumbass.

To get that authentic floral smell, spray the flowers daily with Febreze or your favourite perfume to really bring in the scent of spring!

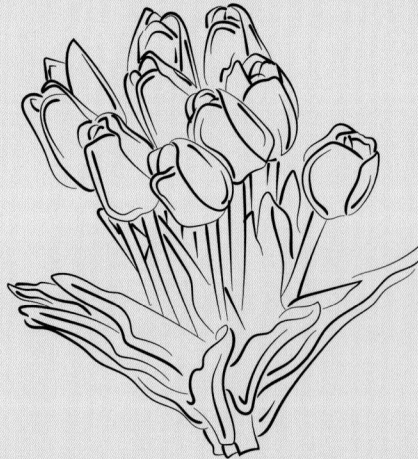

DOUBLE DIP

Fancy yourself a fish pedicure but don't want to splash the cash? Why not make your own pedi-paradise in your back garden with a pretty pond! What's that? You can't be arsed Googling how to build one?

No need to worry, you don't need to be Nick Knowles to make your pond a success.

Turn that DIY SOS into DIY SO-YES using just about anything that holds water - an old storage box, your neighbour's paddling pool, a second-hand coffin... the possibilities are endless!

DECOMPOSE

Got yourself some smelly waste you don't want to keep in your bin? Veggie scraps, sawdust, your ex...
then a compost bin really is the way to go!

You don't need to bother buying a specific bin, just find a plastic or wooden box in some fly-tipper's crap
and drill in some holes. Even easier, the dig and drop method!

Simply dig a hole in your garden, tip in your waste and pat it over... perfect for hiding potato peels
and dead bodies!

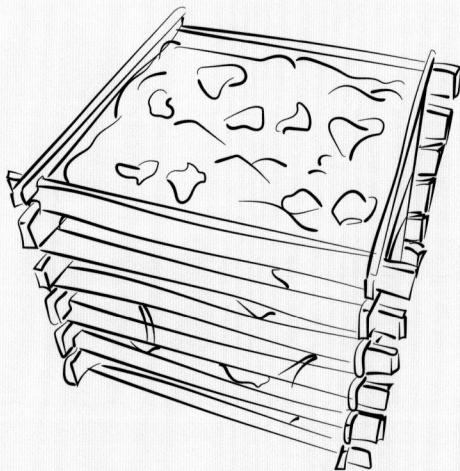

EIGHT-LEGGED FREAKS!

Spiders. Creepy, ugly, eight-legged freaks! Creeping around with their hairy little bodies and 20,000 eyeballs. They enter your home looking for a juicy fly or dusty corner to build their web, squatting in your property rent-free. The audacity!

Living your life in constant fear stops now! Those soggy leaves, twigs and random logs in your garden? Put them in the corner furthest away from your house.

This will be a brand new apartment complex, specifically for spiders, slugs, and woodlice.
(Hedgehogs will make a feast out of them!)

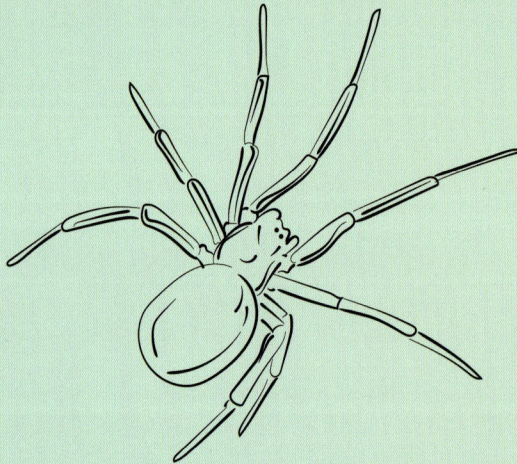

DON'T BE A TIT!

Are you a proud tit lover? Know a great pair when you see them? Or has a lack of tits in your garden left you feeling blue?

Fear not - that broken down fence panel can help you attract tits of all shapes and sizes into your garden!

Simply stack piles of wood or cardboard boxes to make a great home for them, and encourage tits to nest throughout the year! When it comes to tits, enjoy them from a distance... you can look but you can't touch!

ALWAYS USE PROTECTION

We've all been there: you were expecting a summer of love as you begin to enter your prime, but have been left with boxes upon boxes of expired condoms, flooding your room with shame and disappointment.

Did you know that condoms make great vessels to carry water? Why not use one as a makeshift watering can?

A single Johnny can hold up to 2 litres of water! Simply fill it up, tie the end, and unleash your load over your garden! At least then, something is getting wet (even if it's not you...).

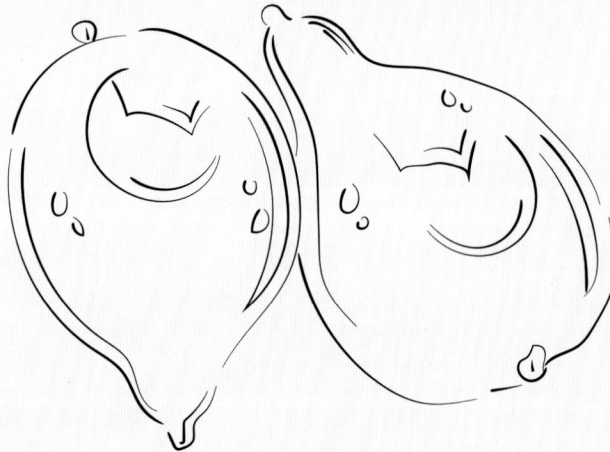

DUSKY DECKING

Picture this: you've woken up, had an epiphany, and no longer want to smother yourself in three coats of extra-dark tan in a can every morning.

Well, here's an idea: why not use your extra tan to stain any old, faded decking or fencing! Just because you don't want a fresh coat of paint doesn't mean your garden deserves to be neglected!

An easy way to bring your backyard into the 21st century, soon your garden will have the gorgeous Essex glow it always wanted!

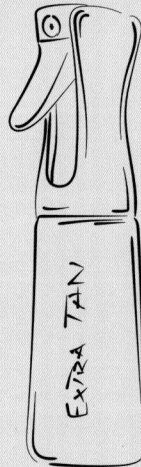

PUSSY PATROL

Have you failed to establish any sort of emotional connection with a human so far in life, and so have filled the loneliness with cats?

Well, I hate to break it to you, but you may be encouraging murder. Your furry feline friends are definitely not a garden's best friend!

Cats attack innocent animals such as birds, mice and frogs that are drawn to your overgrown haven, so keep them indoors to minimise garden genocide. Maybe it's time to cast off your cats and redownload the dating apps, if you actually care about the environment, that is.

GET PISSED

Ever shouted at someone for pissing all over your grass? Best get writing up some apology notes.

Human urine contains high levels of nitrogen, potassium and phosphorous, all of which are excellent nutrients for plants and soil. You also have a constant supply of wee, so this fertiliser for your wildgarden comes at no extra cost.

If you don't mind a slight tangy scent in the summer, pissing on your plants could be a great way to grow your garden!
Top tip: Watch out for nettles.

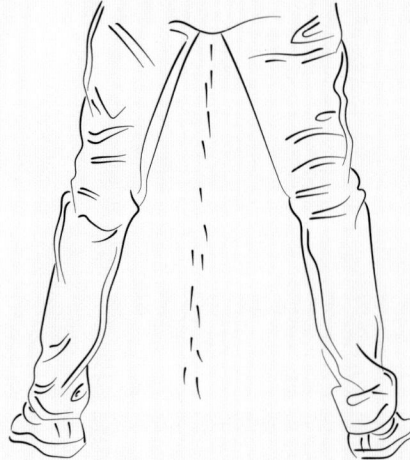

BAG IT UP

If you've been walking around your neighbourhood and have seen small bags that are ghosts of dodgy dealings past littered on the pavement, don't try to ignore them.

Pick them up and give them a quick rinse to repurpose these for storing all your seeds! Ideal for budding gardeners with commitment issues, these are a free way to get organised and start your gardening journey!

HANGING BRA-SKET

Everyone has a bra that just doesn't hold their puppies like it used to. Perhaps you want to spice things up with some saucy lingerie, and are left with some boring bras that you want to throw out!

Before you head to the bin, stitch up the bottom of your bra or granny pants, to use them as makeshift hanging baskets!

Whack them on a hanger and fill with flowers to bring some quirky life back into your dying garden. Wash them before use though... sweaty tit smell isn't something you want in your garden.

ALAN TITCHMARSH

If you're newly knocked up, and find yourself with a pair of leaky lumps, don't let your baby be greedy and suck out all the goodness... save some for your garden!

Did you know that the nutrients in breastmilk are great for your plants, and act as a natural fertiliser? Breast milk can be added to water to help give your plants a little boost all throughout the year!

Try to keep this to yourself... no one wants to see Alan Titchmarsh's lactating nipples on BBC2 anytime soon, unless you're into that kind of thing.

GET CULTURED!

People can talk till the cows come home about the health benefits of probiotic yoghurt, but it doesn't change the fact that it tastes like s**t. YUCKult... am I right?

However, these small yoghurty drinks are a game changer in the world of landscape gardening! Pour it over some rocks and wrap them in cling film to transform your rocky lumps into mossy mounds on the cheap!

After a few days, all kinds of things will be growing, turning your dumping ground into a Zen garden! This tip also works with Greek and natural yoghurt and... petit filous?

UNBREAK MY HEART...

Look. Things happen. One too many beers can naturally lead to a few smashed plant pots. Smashed pots and boozy summer BBQs go hand in hand at this rate.

Don't shove them in the bin! Use a sharpie to mark these shards and turn them into makeshift plant markers! Great for herbs and vegetables, stick them in the soil to let you know what is planted where, because if you keep drinking the way you have been, you'll probably forget.

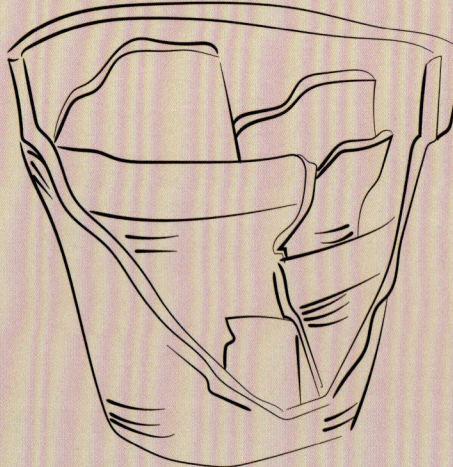

IMPROVISE. ADAPT. OVERCOME.

Is your garden just a lost cause, filled with debris and weeds to such an extent that it seems beyond saving? Well... it probably is. Many people say you can't polish a turd, but you may as well try!

Why not fill your garden with gnomes and ornaments to distract the eye from mounds of rubbish? Try to light some citronella candles to get rid of the stench of rotting food!

Even try turning the overgrown plants and hedges into a fun, family-friendly maze or snug chill out spot! Remember, it's not about what you have, it's about how you use it.

SUCKERS!

Want to get your spook on this autumn, or maybe you just want to keep chavs and charity volunteers away?

Whatever your reason, you can turn your dreary brick house into a castle fit for a bloodsucking vampire! With a spooky bat house, you can make the burliest of men squeal and sob.

You don't even need to buy one, just hammer a wooden box to the wall of your home, and no more will charity workers sneak up your path, asking you to donate your life savings or become a blood donor!

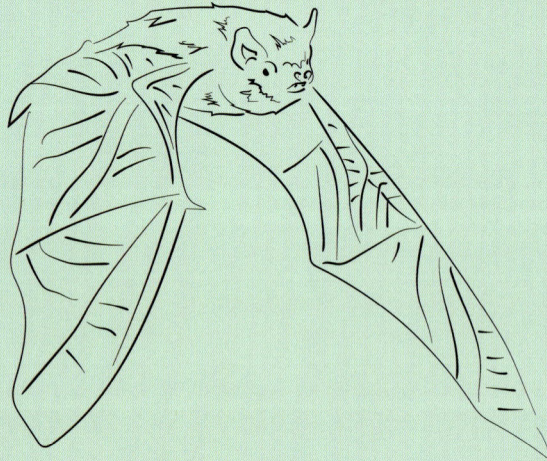

EX-ESSORIES!

Have you just kicked your arsehole ex out of your house and are about to shred or burn their clothes?

STOP!

Don't waste precious garden accessories just because they're a twat, put them to good use!

Their shoes are your new plant pots, their shirt is now your new peg bag, and their jeans, well... they fit your flowers much better anyway!

FLOWER BUD LIGHT

Is your garden littered with empty cans of lager after the last bank holiday weekend?

Why not make them a permanent feature in your splendidly common garden?

From a dedicated tab-end container, to plant pots and even dangling them from trees just to piss off some shitty birds, your battered tins of Carling, Becks or Bud Light are sure to bring up the market value of your housing estate!

PAN-SCAPES

You've just finished your dinner and now have three pans full of cloudy water and soggy broccoli bits, but your sink is full of washing up that will be there for another day or so.

What do you do? While you might look like you've just escaped from your local mental asylum, pouring pans of water around your garden is a sure way to get your garden growing!

Don't try it with pasta water though, or your dandelions will join the Italian Mafia...
(They're always listening!)

STINGER FOR LOVE

Sick of nosey Moreen walking up your drive, just to talk about last night's episode of Corrie or when you're planning on trimming your overgrown bushes?

No need to buy an ankle-biting Chihuahua to deter unwanted guests, nettles are the new in-thing!

These stabby fiends are not only great for avoiding social contact, they can also be brewed into tea or eaten like spinach!

LET IT GROW!

Why mow your lawn when you're going to have to do it again in a few weeks' time?

Lugging around a big-ass lawnmower and getting pissed off when you can't quite reach the edges, resulting in you having to bring out the noisy strimmer too. Think smart and skip the trim!

If you stop trimming your lawn altogether, then it can only grow back once. Your neighbours can't get mad at your luscious jungle either, since you're saving them the pain of listening to you mow!

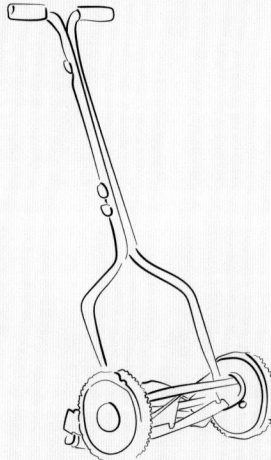

BIG BLOOMERS!

Flowers are great. They can make a crap-filled garden look so much more beautiful and majestic.

Who cares if you've got a dresser, toilet, and washing machine slung across your yard? Just implement them into the landscape.

That toilet makes for a fabulous new planter, the dresser can be shelving for your little pots, and that washing machine, well say hello to your brand new garden table!

A HELPING HAND

Is your garden lacking personality? Much like yourself, gardens need a personal touch to complete the look.

Don't worry though, you don't need to pay an arm and a leg for fancy decorations from the garden centre, just nick yourself a Primark mannequin, dismember it, and spread its limbs around your flowerbeds.

Your garden will look like a contemporary art museum, and your neighbours will stay far, far away from you. Win, win!

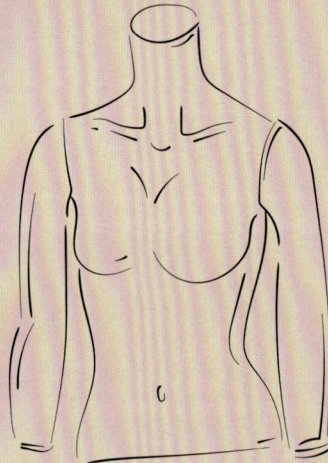

UP THE WALL!

Does that odd brickwork drive you up the wall? The builder who fixed up your home was quite obviously colour-blind, using orange bricks on a red house (tut, tut).

There's a way to hide that cowboy build though, and it doesn't involve using a hammer or paint. Find yourself some creepy crawling plants like ivy, and you can make your home look like a magnificent cottage!

Just beware of the insects it might attract. Oh, and that spider in your hair!

AIM HIGH

Think your garden is too 'high' maintenance? Stop prodding and pruning your lawn and pathway, and let the weeds grow!

A plant that doesn't require potting, not only will it add a dash of colour to your driveway, it'll make your lawn look thicker, and even entice daisies and dandies to grow!

Just don't grow the real thing, or you might get busted!

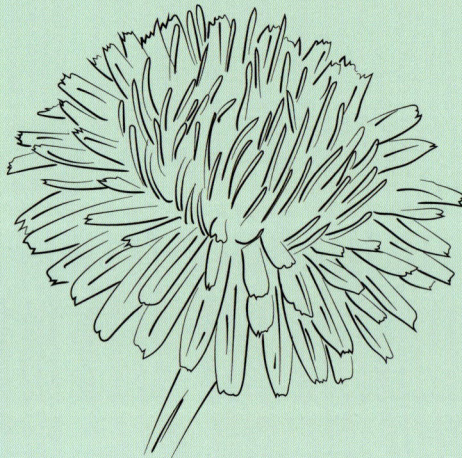

UGLY DUCKLING

Who said weeds are ugly? It's the 2000's, so drop the beauty standards, because some weeds are prettier than your average garden plant! The knapweed for example, ugly name right?

But this weed stands tall and proud, blooming beautifully in pink and purple.

So next time you're called ugly, grow like the weed you are!

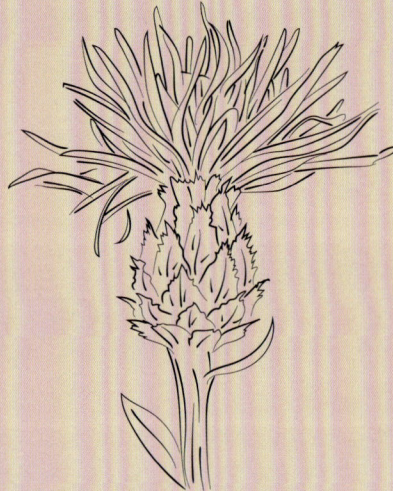

SUPERMARKET SWEEP

Everyone can admire the beauty of a housing estate. Shoes dangling from telephone wires, graffiti covering every flat surface, and smashed bottles on every street corner.

There is one item though, which defines a great estate. Shopping trolleys. Yes, these handy little baskets on wheels, which get pinched by little scruffs in tracksuits, really enhance the beauty of their surroundings.

Next time you see a rogue trolley, take it back to your home and fill it with plant pots, garden tools or even just other crap you find on the streets.

SCARECROWS DO HAVE BRAINS

Want to scare away seagulls, pigeons and crows from a certain spot in your garden?

Your home and garden is full of items you can recycle to make your very own bird scarer.

Empty crisp packets rustling in the wind, scrunched up foil, and your S Club 7 CD are all great to hang up on a washing line or branch to scare away birds!

COOL BEANS

The cost of shopping is extortionate these days, so it's always best to use and reuse.

Those chewy budget beans from Aldi? Once you've had your beans on toast, why not wash out the can and reuse it as a tab-end can for your doorstep!

Alternatively, you could use this tin to burn your pyramid scheme candles, or make a miniature air raid shelter for frogs!

LIFE IS A ROLLER COASTER

Have you spotted your neighbour getting their guttering replaced? Get your arse over there and pinch their old pipes! Who cares if it has a small crack in it? It's free!

There's no limits to what you can use them for either. You can poorly nail them to your fence to make a shabby planter, use them to drain puddles when it rains, or even use them to make a theme park for frogs, worms and snails!

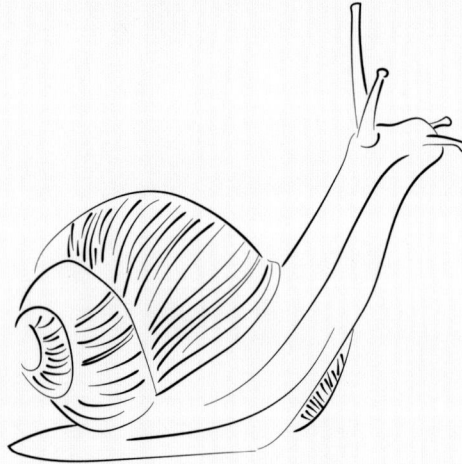

BEE LIVES MATTER

Don't be a serial-killer, poison is for pussies!

Pesticides and insecticides might help get rid of certain pesky creatures, but you're taking along the nice ones too!

Killing off honeybees, ladybirds and hedgehogs in a bid to reduce slugs, rats and greenflies in your home and garden, really does make you a horrible human. Have you never watched Bee Movie?

SEND NOODS

Your favourite plant's stalk snapped in half? Gnome's head fallen off? Life falling to pieces?!

Noodles can fix it! You've seen the videos. Mending holes in doors, tables and sinks using nothing more than MSG filled squiggles of dough. Why not put it into practice?

Wet your noodles and wrap them around the stalk so it can bond together again, use noodles and glue to fix your decapitated gnome, and buy a dozen super noodles to fill that black abyss in your life.

COME TO THE BARK SIDE

Sick of seeing mud and concrete when you step outside? Why not change it up a bit with some bark?

You don't have to mow it frequently, it hides dog poop well, its texture and colour really tidies up your cheap little garden, and it can be home to wood loving creatures like woodlice, centipedes and spiders!

What more could you ask for from dead pieces of tree?

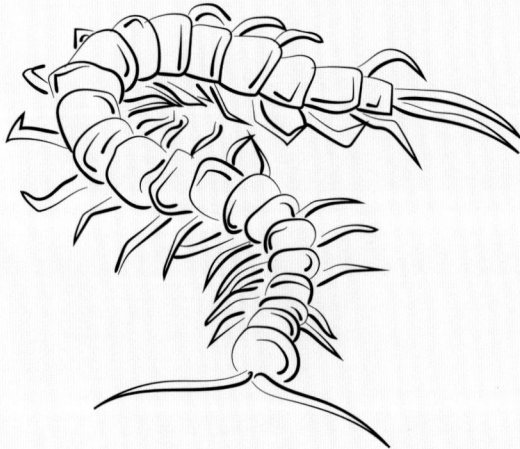

THE BUZZ AROUND TOWN

Not everything that buzzes is a wasp. Bees, hoverflies and vibrators all have a distinct buzzing that can leave us trembling. But can you tell the difference between a wasp and a hoverfly?

Both black and yellow, hoverflies are basically the nice cousins to the wasp. They don't sting, and can actually boost wildlife sightings in your garden.

Their larvae can even fix your bug problem, as they feed on common garden pests. These insects really are a girl's new best friend!

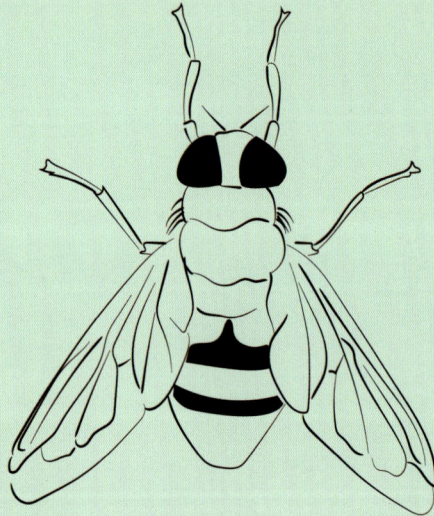

DON'T BUG ME

Ladybirds might seem sweet and innocent, but they are actually ruthless garden security.

Though greedy, they're friends of our gardens, feeding on pesky pests that terrorise our crops and annoy the hell out of us humans.

They crap out yellow toxins when threatened, which deters greenflies and spider mites. They also like to 'get it on', laying hundreds of eggs at a time!

DON'T STOP AND SMELL THE ROSES

Dogs poo in the garden, so why can't humans? Human turds are actually full of nitrogen, phosphorous and potassium, which allows plants to be better nourished and healthier (even if it does smell like a sewer).

No s**t, human crap has been used for centuries to make veggies and flowers bloom and prosper! Toilet roll will decompose in the soil too, so dig yourself a hole in your flowerbed and let one drop, your plants will thank you!

THE TWILIGHT GARDEN

Been watching too many horror films and now you're scared that twinkling vampires will come to your house?

Rather than going through the hassle of digging out your old wooden stakes like Buffy, defend yourself with garlic!

This tasty vegetable has the power to banish Twilight vamps, entice Italian chefs and if turned into a spray, can help keep bacteria and harmful fungus away from your plants!

GOT A SCREW LOOSE

Has your car been dropping loads of rusty bolts and screws lately? I'm sure it's nothing to worry about, probably just your brakes failing or your engine falling out.

When you've got a screw loose, the best thing to do is put it into water for a few days and then water your plants.

The rust releases iron, which is great for making your plants grow and bloom. Just don't go pinching your neighbour's screws, or they'll be sending the men in white coats.

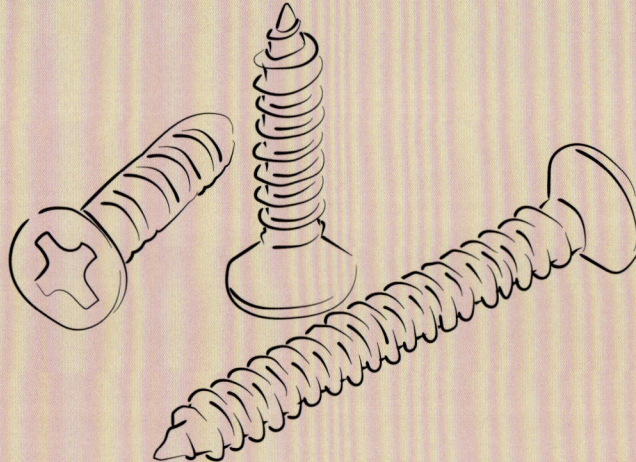

BUMP N' GRIND

World's worst hangover? On your 6th cup of coffee? If you're posh enough to have a coffee grinder, used coffee grounds can be good for your garden too!

Coffee grounds, both used and unused, are great for your soil and garden in general, simply chuck them on your lawn or flower beds to help reduce your waste!

If you can't be arsed to do that even, just whack them on a compost heap, or toss them over your fence to help your lucky neighbours out!

GET STUFFED!

If you've been trimming your bush, and found a deceased member of the local wildlife, don't put it in the bin. Honestly - it lived a life too!

Try respecting the dead WHILST exploring a new hobby - taxidermy - fun for all the family! Make a taxidermy pigeon or stuffed rat - once completed, these ornaments are ideal for bringing a piece of the outside into any home.

Also great as an idea for kids parties, build your own taxidermy farm for a chic and fun pastime, whilst honouring the dead with your beautiful creations! It's a win-win...ish.

A BAG FOR LIFE

20p for a carrier bag?! Outrageous! For that price, you really do want to get your money's worth. Why not turn your bag for life into an automatic watering can for your plants?

Just use a coat hanger to hang it up on your washing line, put a pinprick-sized hole into it, and pop your plants underneath. Every time it rains, it'll fill back up.

Just make sure it's a posh bag... you don't want everyone knowing you shop at Aldi!

LET'S RIDE

If your old banger has finally kicked in, or maybe you've finally had your license taken off you - thank god -
repurpose your old car!

Show off to your neighbours with your new, flashy and very expensive garden ornament - a Ford Fiesta!

Perfect for adding a modern touch to your lawn, a car can be great for storing garden tools, or for escaping
the sun on a lovely summer's day - vroom vroom!

WALK OF SHAME

The old man across the street left his walker by your gate again after having yet another senior moment.

Why give it back when it's bound to happen again? Instead, give it a new home in your trashy little garden!

Perfect to stand plant pots on or to drape your washed granny knickers over in a bid to dry them out, you're only limited to your own imagination!

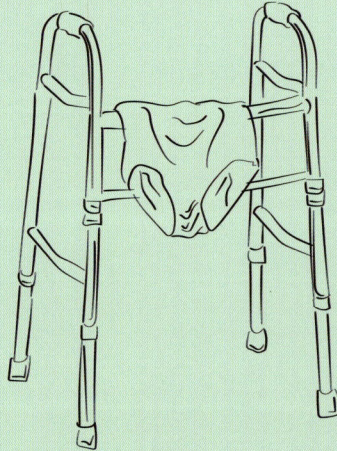

PICTURE THIS!

Has your granny been staring at you from beyond the grave through her dusty old portrait?

Put her outside for a timeout and turn her into an exquisite garden feature!

Doubling as a burgler deterrant, your gran's portrait is sure to give your garden an reminiscent pull to the past!

BALLS TO IT!

Has your neighbour's pesty kids kicked their football into your garden yet again?

Those little swines don't deserve their ball back. If you have a pond, you can use your newly aquired sportsball to save your fish in winter!

Just pop it into the water on an evening, then when the water freezes overnight, you can remove the ball to help the little fishies breathe!

NO JUNK MAIL

Do you sit by your letterbox on a daily basis, hoping to receive your inheritance check from that friendly Nigerian prince? Lets face it, you have no money in your bank account from that 'small' advance payment the prince required, so you could really do with that check.

You're sure to have an abundance of colourful leaflets by now (from churches, blind specialists and takeaways), so why not make use of them to brighten up your garden?

You could make origami flowers out of Luigi's Pizzeria menu, scatter love thy neighbour letters across your path, or pin up Bob's Discount Blinds leaflets to your neighbour's fence as a small hint about their windows!

ABSOLUTELY NO
SOLICITING

EASY AS PEANUTS

Are peanut butter sandwiches your new favourite thing? Can't get enough of that nutty taste?

Why not grow your very own peanut butter! You don't need anything fancy, just an empty butter tub and some soil.

A single plant can grow between 30 and 50 peanuts, and don't need much care at all to grow. When they see your nuts, all your friends will say "I can't believe it's nut butter"!

PEELING HAPPY

Got a lot of banana peels and don't know what to do with them? Banana peels can attract loads of animals into your garden, so why not hang them on your washing line to attract birds and squirrels?

Alternatively, you could play Mario Kart by throwing the peels into the road and watching the chaos commence!

DECK-HEAD

You're going to need a chill out area in your garden, so why not make your wildgarden a-door-able
with DIY decking!

You can make your home more open plan and spacious by removing the doors, and you can place the doors
down on the ground outside to make your very own budget seating space!

Why not remove your kitchen window too, and you can have your very own personal garden bar!

WANNA SPOON?

Has your neighbour been vacuuming all morning and now you're ready for payback? Wind chimes are the perfect accessory for any garden whose owner wants to torture their neighbours.

You can make your very own by tying spoons, forks and butter knifes to a tree or fence. The clattering of metal is sure to make your garden a Zen place to be!

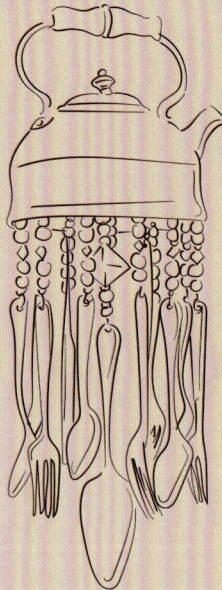

A DICEY DECISION

Always dreamed of visiting Las Vegas but spent all your savings on wax melts and shoes? Why go there when you can bring it here?

If you're an avid gambler, you've probably nabbed a lot of dice and cards over your lifetime. Why not remodel your pathway using concrete, dice and casino chips?

Place your playing cards in plant pots as plant markers and add in a roulette wheel as a bird bath.
Viva Las Garden!

GIVE UP

If your garden gets to the point where it resembles No Man's Land, then there's really no hope in saving it. Give up.

Splurge out and buy yourself some blackout blinds, hide under the table with a cup of coffee and wallow in self pity - who needs a garden anyway?

Roses are shrivelled,
Violets are too.
...I'm a s**t gardener.

books by
BOXER